NEW ZEALAND HORIZONS

PANORAMIC PHOTOGRAPHY BY ANDRIS APSE

craig potton publishing

INTRODUCTION

As is often the case with creative careers, there was a major turning point in Andris Apse's life that marked the beginning of his development as one of New Zealand's pre-eminent landscape photographers. In 1978 he purchased, at what was then an exorbitant price, a Linhof Technorama camera. This enabled him to produce transparencies in a long, extended panoramic format. It quickly proved to be a move of great significance, for it is in this format that Andris found a photographic medium that perfectly suited his sense of composition and his feeling for the spaciousness and breadth of the New Zealand landscape.

Since that time, Andris Apse has tenaciously built a photo collection of extraordinary quality, based around his panoramic photos of the wild and rural landscapes of New Zealand, the kind of landscapes that form the heart of this book.

Characterised by beautifully resolved compositions, intense colour and a highly developed instinct for the dramatic qualities of light, his panoramic photographs have set the benchmark for this style of photography in New Zealand.

An excellent camera and a fine creative eye are not, however, enough to create a photographic career such as that enjoyed by Andris Apse. It takes other things, including a single-minded determination (something he has in abundance) and an abiding and consuming love of his primary subject matter, the New Zealand backcountry. Over the last 20 years he has spent an enormous amount of time combing the rural and wild parts of this country, and his ability and willingness to carry packs loaded with camera gear for extended periods into the wilds of areas such as Fiordland, are legendary.

New Zealand Horizons is but a tiny dip into Andris Apse's photographic collection, but one that will undoubtedly show something of his consummate skill and his love for these wild islands of New Zealand.

Cape Reinga
Whangarei
Coromandel
Auckland
Rotorua
Taupo
New Plymouth
NORTH ISLAND
Napier
Wellington
Nelson
Blenheim
Punakaiki
Kaikoura
Greymouth
SOUTH ISLAND
Franz Josef
Christchurch
Milford Sound
Queenstown
Dunedin
Invercargill
STEWART ISLAND

ABOVE: Evening light on the Pancake Rocks, Punakaiki, West Coast
OVERLEAF: Scotts Beach at the southern end of the Heaphy Track, Kahurangi National Park

ABOVE: The terminal of the Franz Josef Glacier, Westland/Tai Poutini National Park
RIGHT: Lake Matheson, with Mt Tasman and Aoraki/Mt Cook behind, Westland/Tai Poutini National Park
OVERLEAF: Icefall on the névé of the Fox Glacier, Westland/Tai Poutini National Park

LEFT: A rainbow in the canyon of the
Pororari River, inland from Punakaiki,
Paparoa National Park

OVERLEAF: Kahikatea forest and swamp,
with Mt Tasman and Aoraki/Mt Cook
behind, South Westland

ABOVE: Cloud gathers around the peaks above Milford Sound, Fiordland National Park
RIGHT: The setting sun strikes Mitre Peak, Milford Sound, Fiordland National Park

Looking across Hope Arm, Lake Manapouri, Fiordland National Park

Boat on Doubtful Sound, Fiordland National Park

ABOVE: Forest interior, Breaksea Sound, Fiordland National Park
RIGHT: Small stream, Preservation Inlet, Fiordland National Park
OVERLEAF: West Ruggedy Beach on the northwestern tip of Stewart Island

ABOVE: Sheep in the yards, western
Southland

RIGHT: Farmland in the early morning,
Southland

ABOVE: Autumn in the main street of Arrowtown, Central Otago

LEFT: Vineyard overlooking Lake Hayes near Queenstown, Central Otago

ABOVE: The lighthouse at Taiaroa Head, Otago Peninsula
LEFT: Evening over Queenstown, with The Remarkables behind, Central Otago
OVERLEAF: The middle reaches of Lake Hawea, Central Otago

Winter snow on Mt Aspiring and the Bonar Glacier, Mount Aspiring National Park

Dusk at Nugget Point on the Catlins coast, South Otago

ABOVE: Tussock farmland in the Mackenzie Country, South Canterbury
RIGHT: Fishing in the Ahuriri River, South Canterbury high country

ABOVE: Morning light above the Tasman Valley, with Aoraki/Mt Cook behind, Aoraki/Mount Cook National Park
LEFT: Nor'west cloud over Aoraki/Mt Cook and Lake Pukaki, Canterbury

ABOVE: Sheep grazing alongside Lake Coleridge, Canterbury high country

LEFT: Foothills of the Southern Alps, the Rakaia River and the Canterbury Plains

LEFT: Evening light over the head of Lyttelton Harbour, Canterbury

OVERLEAF: Rolling farmland, North Canterbury

ABOVE: Sperm whale diving off the Kaikoura coast

LEFT: Sunrise at Kaikoura, with the Seaward Kaikoura Range behind

OVERLEAF: Autumn in the Brancott Estate Vineyard, Marlborough

ABOVE: Vineyard in the Awatere Valley, with
Mt Tapuae-o-Uenuku behind, Marlborough

RIGHT: Sheep farm near Cape Campbell,
Marlborough

ABOVE: Lake Rotoroa, Nelson Lakes National Park
LEFT: Sunset over the Marlborough Sounds
OVERLEAF: Early morning at Totaranui Beach, Abel Tasman National Park

Marina, Wellington Harbour

Stockman and cattle near Dannevirke, southern Hawke's Bay

Cape Egmont lighthouse, with Mt Taranaki behind

ABOVE: Wai-O-Tapu Thermal Wonderland, Central North Island

LEFT: Evening light over Lake Taupo

OVERLEAF: Mt Ruapehu, Tongariro National Park

Huka Lodge and the Upper Huka Falls on the Waikato River, near Taupo

Tolaga Bay Wharf, East Coast of the North Island

ABOVE: Aerial view over the Waikato River
LEFT: Gorge near Waitomo, King Country
OVERLEAF: Early morning near Otorohanga, southern Waikato

ABOVE: Forest interior, Whirinaki, Central North Island
LEFT: Kauri trees, Waipoua Forest, Northland

ABOVE: Cathedral Cove, Coromandel
Peninsula

RIGHT: Coromandel Harbour, on the
western side of the Coromandel Peninsula

OVERLEAF: Pohutukawa trees, Coromandel
Peninsula

Aerial view of the Harbour Bridge and the Waitemata Harbour, Auckland

Yachts on the Waitemata Harbour, with North Head and Rangitoto Island behind, Auckland

ABOVE: Piercy Island off Cape Brett, Bay of Islands
LEFT: Waewaetorea Island, Bay of Islands
OVERLEAF: Entrance to the Hokianga Harbour, Northland

Sunrise over Rangitoto Island, Auckland

Lighthouse at Cape Reinga, Northland

This edition first published in 2011 by
Craig Potton Publishing,
98 Vickerman Street, PO Box 555,
Nelson, New Zealand

© Andris Apse

ISBN 978-1-877517-37-2

Printed in China by Midas Printing International Ltd

Surfcasting in the Hokianga Harbour,
Northland